Fortune Favors the Bold

365 Inspirational Quotes for Entrepreneurs

Jack Burkhart

Copyright ©2000-2017 Jack Burkhart
Published by OpporTunaMedia, an imprint of
CordaNobeloMedia, printed by Createspace.com.
Publisher can be reached at
Publisher@CordaNobelo.com.

Library of Congress Cataloging-in-Publication Data:
for ordering information see back cover.

**Collect all 4 books in the "Inspirations for
Entrepreneurs" Series:**
"The Quotable Entrepreneur"
"Shake the Damned Tree!"
"Fortune Favors The Bold"
"1001 Inspirational Quotes for Entrepreneurs"

See also www.OpporTunaMedia.com

Acknowledgements

Thanks for everything to all the entrepreneurs I have worked with in Digital People, a large nonprofit for entrepreneurs. Also, to A. David Silver for his inspirational book "The Entrepreneurial Life," to Entrepreneurship Professors Dan Muzyka and Bill Bygrave and, most of all, to Hermann Hauser, Gentleman Entrepreneur.

Thanks also to my father and brother, Max and Torsten.

I have tried to attribute quotations as accurately as I can, and to acknowledge disparate sources. Any errors are honest errors and will be amended immediately you let me know!

Dedicated to entrepreneurs and futurepreneurs worldwide.....

Foreword

For an entrepreneur, Entrepreneurship is a more than way of life; it is a religion. There's just no other conceivable way to exist. Maybe for you, too?

As an entrepreneur in California's Silicon Valley, I had collected these quotes over the years to keep me cheerful. One Christmas, I decided to pull them all together into a book to give my entrepreneur friends for whom I couldn't afford to buy a present.

Years later, I went to visit an entrepreneur friend I had lost contact with and he still had a copy of this book on his bedside table, with coffee rings on it. He said he liked to read a few quotations every evening just before he went to sleep.

That's when I realized that other entrepreneurs like you might find these quotes useful. This is that book.

It was Nelson Mandela, once a prison inmate for 27 years, later President of South Africa and Noble Laureate, who said "The Struggle is my Life". If this rings true for you, then, as a fellow entrepreneur, I salute you!

Enjoy!
Jack Burkhart,
Palo Alto, California.

PS. For more inspirational quotes for entrepreneurs, check out the other books in the "Inspirations for Entrepreneurs" series. **If you think this book is useful for other entrepreneurs, then write a review on your online book retailer, email us your mailing address to publisher@cordanobelo.com and we will mail you another of the books in the series.**

PPS. Some of these quotes are historical, when entrepreneurs were presumably assumed to be exclusively male! Please let nobody be offended and please substitute "she" for "he", as appropriate.

They never told me I couldn't.
Tom Dempsey

I have learned over the years when one's mind is made up, this diminishes fear; knowing what must be done does away with fear.
Rosa Parks

Entrepreneurship is the last refuge of the trouble-making individual.
Natalie Clifford Barney

I have not failed. I've just found 10,000 ways that won't work.
Thomas Edison

Formal education will make you a living; self-education will make you a fortune.
Jim Rohn

The most valuable thing you can make is a mistake – you can't learn anything from being perfect.
Adam Osborne

A man must be big enough to admit his mistakes, smart enough to profit from them, and strong enough to correct them.
John C. Maxwell

Listening is the most powerful weapon after self-belief and persistence you can bring into play as an entrepreneur.
Felix Dennis

Our business in life is not to get ahead of others, but to get ahead of ourselves.
E. Joseph Cossman

Logic will get you from A to B. Imagination will take you everywhere. Albert Einstein

You can't ask customers what they want and then try to give that to them. By the time you get it built, they'll want something new.
Steve Jobs
Live out of your imagination instead of out of your memory.
Fortune Cookie

Success is liking yourself, liking what you do, and liking how you do it.
Maya Angelou

What is robbing a bank compared with founding a bank?
Bertold Brecht

If you are seeking creative ideas, go out walking.
Angels whisper to a man when he goes for a
walk.
Raymond Inman

Success is walking from failure to failure with no
loss of enthusiasm.
Winston Churchill

A man's worth is no greater than the worth of his
ambitions.
Marcus Aurelius

If you cannot do great things, do small things in
a great way.
Napoleon Hill

I don't know the key to success, but the key to
failure is trying to please everybody.
Bill Cosby

There comes a time in a man's life when to get
where he has to go – if there are no doors or
windows – he walks through a wall.
Bernard Malmud

Tell everyone what you want to do and someone will want to help you do it.
W. Clement Stone

Success is not in what you have, but who you are.
Bo Bennett

You're gonna lose some ballgames and you're gonna win some ballgames and that's about it.
Sparky Anderson

Coming together is a beginning; keeping together is progress; working together is success.
Henry Ford

Great achievement is usually born of great sacrifice, and is never the result of selfishness.
Napoleon Hill

Try not to be a man of success, but rather try to become a man of value. Albert Einstein

The best way to predict the future is to create it.
Peter Drucker

You can do anything you wish to do, have anything you wish to have, be anything you wish to be.
Robert Collier

Doctors and scientists said that breaking the four-minute mile was impossible, that one would die in the attempt. Thus, when I got up from the track after collapsing at the finish line, I figured I was dead.
Roger Bannister

A leader is one who knows the way, goes the way, and shows the way.
John C. Maxwell
For every good reason there is to lie, there is a better reason to tell the truth. Bo Bennett

In order to succeed, your desire for success should be greater than your fear of failure.
Bill Cosby

Regardless of who you are or what you have been, you can be what you want to be.
W. Clement Stone

The secret of success in life is for a man to be
ready for his opportunity when it comes.
Benjamin Disraeli

You were born to win, but to be a winner, you must plan to win, prepare to win, and expect to win.
Zig Ziglar

Discipline is the bridge between goals and accomplishment.
Jim Rohn

If you will not believe in yourself, then why should anyone else?
Felix Dennis

Action speaks louder than words but not nearly as often.
Mark Twain

Successful people are always looking for opportunities to help others. Unsuccessful people are asking, What's in it for me?
Brian Tracy

Always listen to experts. They'll tell you what can't be done and why. Then do it.
Robert Heinlein

A goal is a dream with a deadline.
Napoleon Hill

Entrepreneurship is neither a science nor an art.
It is a practice.
Peter Drucker

The function of leadership is to produce more
leaders, not more followers.
Ralph Nader

Act enthusiastic and you will be enthusiastic.
Dale Carnegie

"One can't believe impossible things." "I daresay
you haven't had much practice," said the Queen.
"When I was your age, I always did it for half an
hour a day. Why, sometimes I've believed as
many as six impossible things before breakfast."
Lewis Carroll

You take on the responsibility for making your
dream a reality.
Les Brown

You're only here for a short visit. Don't hurry, don't worry. And be sure to smell the flowers along the way.
Walter Hagen

The superior man is modest in his speech, but exceeds in his actions.
Confucius

One doesn't discover new lands without consenting to lose sight of the shore for a very long time.
André Gide

Don't just read the easy stuff. You may be entertained by it, but you will never grow from it.
Jim Rohn

Tell the world what you intend to do, but first show it.
Napoleon Hill

If you always do what you've always done, you'll always get what you've always got!
Alan Scott

Vision without action is daydreaming and action without vision is a nightmare. Anon

Success is getting what you want. Happiness is wanting what you get.
Dale Carnegie

Without continual growth and progress, such words as improvement, achievement, and success have no meaning.
Benjamin Franklin

If you want to reach a goal, you must "see the reaching" in your own mind before you actually arrive at your goal.
Zig Ziglar

The few who do are the envy of the many who only watch.
Jim Rohn

An ounce of action is worth a ton of theory.
Ralph Waldo Emerson

There is only one success – to be able to spend your life in your own way.
Christopher Morley

The way to get started is to quit talking and begin doing.
Walt Disney

Try, try, try, and keep on trying is the rule that must be followed to become an expert in anything.
W. Clement Stone

Big pay and little responsibility are circumstances seldom found together.
Napoleon Hill

Every choice you make has an end result.
Zig Ziglar

Every man paddle his own canoe.
Frederick Marryat

You won't get anything unless you have the vision to imagine it.
John Lennon

"Never give in" is a useful catchphrase. But don't take it too literally. We must all surrender at some time. But never give in easily. If you can, attempt one step farther down the road than appears sensible before giving in.
Felix Dennis

Ideas can be life-changing. Sometimes all you need to open the door is just one more good idea.
Jim Rohn

If everything seems under control, you're just not going fast enough.
Mario Andretti

Coming together is a beginning. Keeping together is progress. Working together is success.
Henry Ford

Success is the maximum utilization of the ability that you have.
Zig Ziglar

The road to success and the road to failure are almost exactly the same.
Colin R. Davis

Success is how high you bounce after you hit bottom.
General George Patton

If you are going to ask yourself life-changing questions, be sure to do something with the answers.
Bo Bennett

In the modern world of business, it is useless to be a creative, original thinker unless you can also sell what you create.
David Ogilvy

Positive thinking will let you do everything better than negative thinking will.
Zig Ziglar

In the realm of ideas everything depends on enthusiasm. In the real world all rests on perseverance.
Johann Wolfgang von Goethe

Every morning I get up and look through the Forbes list of the richest people in America. If I'm not there, I go to work.
Robert Orben

I've learned that mistakes can often be as good a teacher as success.
Jack Welch

I can accept failure, everyone fails at something. But I can't accept not trying.
Michael Jordan

Face reality as it is, not as it was or as you wish it to be.
Jack Welch

As a rule, we find what we look for; we achieve what we get ready for.
James Cash Penney

Money won't make you happy... but everybody wants to find out for themselves.
Zig Ziglar

It is always the start that requires the greatest effort.
James Cash Penney

If you are not willing to risk the unusual, you will have to settle for the ordinary.
Jim Rohn

If you don't have a competitive advantage, don't compete.
Jack Welch

Happiness is that state of consciousness which proceeds from the achievement of one's values.
Ayn Rand

How wonderful it is that nobody need wait a single moment to improve the world.
Anne Frank

If you can DREAM it, you can DO it.
Walt Disney

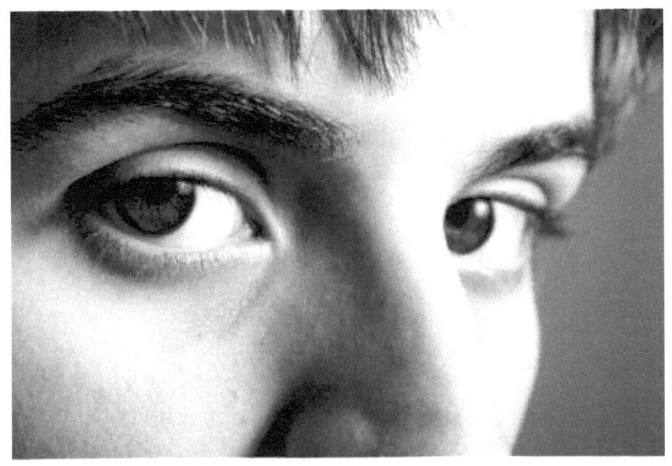

Stubbornness is not persistence. Stubbornness implies you intend to persist despite plentiful evidence that you should not.
Felix Dennis

Buddha left a road map, Jesus left a road map, Krishna left a road map, Rand McNally left a road map. But you still have to travel the road yourself.
Stephen Levine

To change one's life. Start immediately.
Do it flamboyantly. No Exceptions.
William James

If you want to feel rich, just count all of the things you have that money can't buy.
Anon.

It's kind of fun to do the impossible.
Walt Disney

What lies behind us and what lies before us are small matters to what lies within us.
Ralph Waldo Emerson

People are like stained-glass windows. They sparkle and shine when the sun is out, but when the darkness sets in, their true beauty is revealed only if there is a light from within.
Elizabeth Kübler-Ross

And the trouble is, if you don't risk anything, you risk even more.
Erica Jong

A dream is just a dream. A goal is a dream with a plan and a deadline.
Harvey Mackay

Failure is not about insecurity. It's about lack of execution.
Jeffrey Gitomer

Better understated than overstated. Let people be surprised that it was more than you promised and easier than you said.
Jim Rohn

Men often become what they believe themselves to be. If I believe I cannot do something, it makes me incapable of doing it. But when I believe I can, then I acquire the ability to do it even if I didn't have it in the beginning.
Gandhi

No person was ever honored for what he received. Honor has been the reward for what he gave.
Calvin Coolidge

Worry is like a rocking chair: it gives you something to do, but it doesn't get you anywhere.
Dorothy Galyean

Destiny is not a matter of chance, it is a matter of choice. It is not a thing to be waited for, it is a thing to be achieved.
Jeremy Kitson

We would worry less about what others think of us if we realized how seldom they do.
Ethel Barrett

The time is always right to do what is right.
Martin Luther King, Jr.

Success breeds success. Attend to your mind's most joyful, effective discovery process. Bolster the self-beliefs that add confidence, lucidity, and tenacity to your efforts. You'll get more out of what you notice, so heed whatever gives you wisdom.
Marsha Sinetar

I couldn't wait for success, so I went ahead without it.
Jonathan Winters

I'd say it's been my biggest problem all my life.
It's money. It takes a lot of money to make these
dreams come true.
Walt Disney

Ability may get you to the top, but it takes
character to keep you there.
John Wooden

Learn to get in touch with the silence within
yourself, and know that everything in this life has
purpose. There are no mistakes, no coincidences.
All events are blessings given to us to learn from.
Elizabeth Kübler-Ross

All the darkness in the world cannot put out the
light of a single candle.
Unknown

Nothing great was ever achieved without
enthusiasm.
Ralph Waldo Emerson
Think big, act small. A successful and naturally
modest entrepreneur is an object of reverence
and respect in the business world.
Felix Dennis

I learned this, at least, by my experiment: that if one advances confidently in the direction of his dreams, and endeavors to live the life which he had imagined, he will meet with a success unexpected in common hours.
Henry David Thoreau

Whatever you can do or dream you can, begin it. Boldness has genius, power, and magic in it. Begin it now.
Goethe

I have often been adrift, but I have always
stayed afloat.
David Berry

Plodding wins the race
Aesop

I think there is something more important than
believing: Action! The world is full of dreamers.
There aren't enough who will move ahead and
take concrete steps to actualize their vision.
W. Clement Stone

When you get into a tight place and everything
goes against you, 'til it seems as though you
could not hang on a minute longer, never give up
then, for it is just the place and time that the tide
will turn.
Harriet Beecher Stowe

Most of the shadows of this life are caused by
standing on one's own sunshine.
Ralph Waldo Emerson

You can't make someone else's choices. You
shouldn't let someone else make yours.
General Colin Powell

Perfection is achieved, not when there is nothing
left to add, but when there is nothing left to take
away.
Antoine de St. Exupery

You will do foolish things, but do them with enthusiasm.
Colette

Begin somewhere; you cannot build a reputation on what you intend to do.
Liz Smith

You may have to fight a battle more than once to win it.
Margaret Thatcher

God gives us talent; work transforms talent into genius.
Anna Pavlova

Getting rich comes from an attitude of mind. It isn't going to happen if things drift on pretty much the way they are right now.
Felix Dennis

Success is never permanent; failure is never fatal. The only thing that really counts is to never, never, never give up.
Sir Winston Churchill

You gain strength, courage and confidence by every experience in which you really stop to look fear in the face... You must do the thing which you think you cannot do.
The future belongs to those who believe in the beauty of their dreams.
Eleanor Roosevelt

I want to do it because I want to do it.
Amelia Earhart

It had long since come to my attention that people of accomplishment rarely sat back and let things happen to them. They went out and happened to things.
Elinor Smith

It doesn't matter what you are thinking or what fear you have, if you just do it. Action is the only thing that matters. I can see that at the end of my life, I'm going to look back and say, "Gosh, I wish I had taken more action."
Diana von Welanetz Wentworth

Your most unhappy customers are your greatest source of learning.
Bill Gates

If you do build a great experience, customers tell each other about that. Word of mouth is very powerful.
Jeff Bezos

Many great ideas go unexecuted, and many great executioners are without ideas. One without the other is worthless.
Tim Blixseth

I've always worked very, very hard, and the harder I worked, the luckier I got.
Alan Bond

Make your product easier to buy than your competition, or you will find your customers buying from them, not you.
Mark Cuban

Doubt, of whatever kind, can be ended by action alone.
Thomas Carlyle

In order to change, we must be sick and tired of being sick and tired.
Anon.

If at first you don't succeed, try, try, try again.
W.E. Hickson

Whenever you see a successful business,
someone once made a courageous decision.
Peter Drucker

You can't expect to hit the jackpot if you don't
put some nickels in the machine.
Flip Wilson

"Mean to" don't pick no cotton.
Anon.

Above all, try something.
Franklin D. Roosevelt.

Do it big, or stay in bed.
Larry Kelly

Let us be brave in the face of adversity.
Seneca

I do not believe a man can ever leave his
business. He ought to think of it by day and
dream of it by night.
Henry Ford

He's no failure. He's not dead yet.
W. L. George.

Continuous effort – not strength or intelligence –
is the key to unlocking our potential
Sir Winston Churchill.

Only those who dare to fail greatly can ever
achieve greatly.
Robert F Kennedy

It is the business of the future to be dangerous.
Alfred North Whitehead

What counts is not necessarily the size of the dog
in the fight, but the size of the fight in the dog.
Dwight. D. Eisenhower.

Anyone can hold the helm when the sea is calm.
Publius Syrus.

Forget mistakes. Forget failure. Forget everything except what you're going to do now and do it. Today is your lucky day.
Will Durant

Entrepreneurs average 3.9 failures before final success. What sets the successful ones apart is their amazing persistence. There are a lot of people out there with good and marketable ideas, but pure entrepreneurial types almost never accept defeat.
Lisa M Amos

You'll never find a better sparring partner than adversity.
Walt Schmidt.

We learn courageous action by going forward whenever fear urges us to go back. A little boy was asked how he learned to skate. "By getting up every time I fell down," he answered.
David Seabury

You will perceive just how much money there is in the world and how pitifully easy it is to obtain it. Money that already has your name on it.
Felix Dennis

Life affords no higher pleasures than that of surmounting difficulties.
Samuel Johnson

A problem well stated is a problem half solved.
Charles F Kettering.
We must dare, and dare again, and go on daring.
Georges Jacques Danton

It's just another crisis
Rupert M. Hart

Failure is an event, not a person.
William D Brown

We should not let our fears hold us back from pursuing our hopes.
John F Kennedy

Change is what people fear most.
Fyodor Dostoyevsky

One ought never to turn one's back on a threatened danger and try to run away from it. If you do that, you will double any danger. But if you meet it promptly and without flinching, you will reduce the danger by half. Never run away from anything. Never!
Sir Winston Churchill

The future is here. It's just not evenly distributed yet.
William Gibson

Of all the sad words of tongue or pen, the saddest are these: It might have been.
John Greenleaf Whittier

There is no data on the future.
Laurel Cutler

Everyone gets their rough day. No one gets a free ride. Today so far, I had a good day. I got a dial tone.
Rodney Dangerfield.

We must dare to have unthinkable thoughts.
James W Fulbright.

I'm in wonderful position: I'm unknown, I'm underrated, and there's nowhere to go but up.
Pierre DuPont IV

It is the greatest shot of adrenaline to be doing what you've wanted to do so badly. You almost feel like you could fly without the plane.
Charles Lindbergh

Morale is the greatest single factor in successful wars.
Dwight D. Eisenhower

I have always been delighted at the prospect of a new day, a fresh try, one more start, worth perhaps a bit of magic waiting somewhere behind the morning.
J. B. Priestley

Bravery is the capacity to perform properly even when scared half to death.
General Omar Bradley

Behold the turtle. He makes progress only when he sticks his neck out.
James Conant

Grant me the courage not to give up even though
I think it is hopeless.
Chester W Nimitz

A leader is a dealer in hope.
Napoleon Bonaparte

Let me tell you the secret that has led me to my
goal. My strength lies solely in my tenacity.
Louis Pasteur

To keep a lamp burning we have to keep putting
oil in it.
Mother Teresa

Failure is something made only by those who fail
to dare, not by those who dare to fail.
Anne Morrow Lindbergh

Entrepreneurship – the most fun you can have
with your clothes on.
Anon.

Never confuse a single defeat with final defeat.
F. Scott Fitzgerald.

Success is going from failure to failure without
loss of enthusiasm.
Sir Winston Churchill

Don't look forward to the day when you stop
suffering. Because when it comes, you'll know
you're dead.
Tennessee Williams

Many a man never fails because he never tries.
Norman MacEwan

Without hope men are only half alive. With hope
they dream and think and work.
Charles Sawyer.

The pessimist sees the difficulty in every
opportunity; the optimist sees the opportunity in
every difficulty.
L.P.Jacks

My center is giving way, my right is in retreat:
situation excellent. I am attacking.
Marshal Foch

What if everything went right?
Zen

You must avoid the trap of going into what you
think will make you money if you have no
empathy or feeling for what you are about to do.

Felix Dennis

Enthusiasm can only be aroused by two things: first, an ideal which takes the imagination by storm, and second, a definite intelligible plan for carrying that ideal into practice.
Arnold Toynbee

Nothing happens unless first a dream
Carl Sandburg

Decision and determination are the engineer and fireman of our train to opportunity and success.
Burt Lawlor

Trust your own instinct. Your mistakes might as well be your own, instead of someone else's.
Billy Wilder

Be like a postage stamp – stick to one thing 'til you get there.
Josh Billings

If you break your neck, if you have nothing to eat, if your house is on fire – then you got a problem. Everything else is inconvenience.
Robert Fulghum

To love what you do and feel that it matters –
how could anything else be more fun?
Katherine Graham

Eighty percent of success is showing up.
Woody Allen

The tragedy of life is not that it ends so soon, but
that we wait so long to begin it.
Anon.

The wave of the future is coming and there is no
fighting it.
Anne Morrow Lindbergh

It is the lone worker who makes the first advance
in a subject: the details may be worked out by a
team, but the prime idea is due to the enterprise,
thought and perception of an individual.
Sir Alexander Fleming
Discoverer of penicillin

Many strokes overthrow the tallest oak.
John Lyly

There is nothing more difficult to take in hand, more perilous to conduct, or more uncertain in its success, than to take the lead in the introduction of a new order of things.
Niccolo Machiavelli

Courage is not the absence of fear but the
mastery of it.
Mark Twain

Men do not fail; they stop trying.
Elihu Root.

In embracing change, entrepreneurs ensure
social and economic stability.
George Gilder.

Too busy with the crowded hour to fear to live or
die.
Ralph Waldo Emerson

Some days you tame the tiger. And some days
the tiger has you for lunch.
Tug McGraw.

Vision is the art of seeing the invisible.
Jonathan Swift

Call the roll in your memory of conspicuously
successful business giants and ...you will be
struck by the fact that almost every one of them
encountered inordinate difficulties sufficient to
crush all but the gamest of spirits. Edison went
hungry many times before he became famous.
B. C. Forbes

To know just what has to be done, then to do it, comprises the whole philosophy of practical life.
Sir William Osler

The key to everything is patience. You get the chicken by hatching the egg – not by smashing it.
Arnold Glasgow

Trouble is only opportunity in work clothes.
Henry J Kaiser

To strive, to seek, to find, and not to yield.
Alfred Lord Tennyson

None of us can be free of conflict and woe. Even the greatest men have had to accept disappointments as their daily bread.
Bernard M Baruch

Hope is the last thing that dies in a man.
Francois de la Rochefoucault

If you do what you've always done, you'll get what you've always gotten.
Anon.

You cannot step twice into the same river.
Heraclitus.

Choosing a goal and sticking to it changes
everything.
Scott Reed

We are all in the gutter, but some of are looking
at the stars.
Oscar Wilde.

True happiness...is not attained through self-
gratification, but through fidelity to a worthy
purpose.
Helen Keller

What is more mortifying than to feel that you
have missed the plum for want of courage to
shake the tree?
Logan Pearsall Smith

Don't wait for your ship to come; swim to it.
Anon.

You cannot banish fear, but you can face it down, stomp on it, crush it, bury it, padlock it into the deepest recesses of your heart and soul and leave it there to rot.
Felix Dennis

Effort only fully releases its reward after a person refuses to quit.
Napoleon Hill

Life has no smooth road for any of us.
W. C. Doane

Destiny is what you are supposed to do in life. Fate is what kicks you in the ass to make you do it.
Henry Miller

Failure is not in losing, but in no longer believing that winning is worthwhile.
Anon.

Far and away the best prize that life offers is the chance to work hard at work worth doing.
Theodore Roosevelt

The best way out of a problem is through it.
Anon.

It's no good running a pig farm badly for thirty years while saying "Really I was meant to be a ballet dancer." By that time, pigs will be your style.
Quentin Crisp

I have no private life. I have a wife who understands. When the phone doesn't ring at home I get depressed. So my wife says "Why not go out and sell something, Lew?" And that always cheers me up.

Lord Lew Grade

Media Magnate

A winner never quits, and a quitter never wins.
Anon.

You cannot fight against the future. Time is on
our side.
William Gladstone

A musician must make magic, an artist must
paint, a poet must write, if he is to be ultimately
at peace with himself. What a man can be, he
must be.
Abraham Maslow

Order and simplification are the first steps toward
the mastery of a subject – the actual enemy is
the unknown.
Thomas Mann

Dare to be naïve.
Buckminster Fuller

But I, being poor, have only my dreams;
I have spread my dreams under your feet; Tread
softly because you tread on my dreams.
William Butler Yeats

All progress is based upon a universal innate desire on the part of every organism to live beyond its income.
Samuel Butler

In a calm sea every man is a pilot.
John Ray

An institution is the lengthened shadow of one man.
Ralph Waldo Emerson

Discovery consists of seeing what everybody has seen and thinking what nobody has thought.
Albert Szent-Gyorgi

The will to do, the soul to dare.
Sir Walter Scott
The Lady of the Lake

He wants to leave a scratch on that wall – Kilroy was here – that somebody a hundred, or a thousand years later will see.
William Faulkner

The cat in gloves catches no mice
Benjamin Franklin

'Twixt the optimist and pessimist
The difference is droll
The optimist sees the doughnut
But the pessimist sees the hole.
McLandburgh Wilson

There is the greatest practical benefit in making a
few failures early in life
Thomas Huxley

I am the master of my fate,
I am the captain of my soul.
William Ernest Henley
Echoes

Each problem has hidden in it an opportunity so
powerful that it literally dwarfs the problem. The
greatest success stories were created by people
who recognized a problem and turned it into an
opportunity.
Joseph Sugarman

I've got a great ambition to die of exhaustion
rather than boredom.
Angus Grossart

Innovations come from creative destruction.
Yoshihisa Tabuchi

To be successful, keep looking tanned, live in an elegant building (even if you're in the cellar), be seen in smart restaurants (even if you nurse one drink) and if you borrow, borrow big.
Aristotle Onassis

The only truth about Luck, good or bad, is that it will change.
Felix Dennis

They can because they think they can.
Virgil

To the timid and hesitating everything is impossible because it seems so.
Sir Walter Scott

A great manager has a knack of making ballplayers think they are better than they think they are. He forces you to have a good opinion of yourself. He lets you know he believes in you. He makes you get more out of yourself. And once you learn how good you really are, you never settle for playing anything less than your very best.
Reggie Jackson

If you've got it, flaunt it. If you do not, pretend.
Wally Phillips

They've got us surrounded again, the poor bastards.
Gen George Creighton W Abrams

Courage is being scared to death...and saddling up anyway.
John Wayne

We shall draw from the heart of suffering itself the means of inspiration and survival.
Sir Winston Churchill

The moment one definitely commits oneself,
Providence moves too. All sorts of things occur to
help, that would never otherwise have occurred.
W. H. Murray

Choices are the hinges of destiny.
Edwin Markham

Nature's mighty law is change.
Robert Burns

You have to have a dream so you wake up in the morning.
Billy Wilder.

The world stands aside to let anyone pass who knows where he is going.
David Starr Jordan

Whatever course you have chosen for yourself, it will not be a chore but an adventure if you bring to it a sense of the glory of striving, if your sights are set far above the merely secure and mediocre.
David Sarnoff

Do what you love and the money will follow.
Marsha Sinetar

Every successful person I have heard of has done the best he could with the conditions as he found them, and not waited until next year for better.
E W Howe

It takes twenty years to make an overnight success.
Eddie Cantor

As long as you can start, you are all right. The juice will come.
Ernest Hemingway

Pick battles big enough to matter, small enough to win.
Jonathan Kozol

Life is pretty simple: You do some stuff. Most fails. Some works. You do more of what works. If it works big, others quickly copy it. Then you do something else. The trick is the doing of something else.
Tom Peters

If at first you don't succeed, you're running about average.
M H Alderson

The only history that is worth a tinker's damn is what we make today.
Henry Ford

The most important thing in communication is to hear what isn't being said.
Peter F. Drucker

If what you are doing is not moving you towards your goals, then it's moving you away from your goals.
Brian Tracy

The entrepreneur builds an enterprise; the technician builds a job.
Michael Gerber

As long as you're going to be thinking anyway, think big.
Donald Trump

Don't make friends who are comfortable to be with. Make friends who will force you to lever yourself up.
Thomas J. Watson

All achievements, all earned riches, have their beginning in an idea.
Napoleon Hill

Commuter – one who spends life
In riding to and from his wife;
A man who shaves and takes a train
And then rides back to shave again
E.B White
"Commuter"

We all live in a state of ambitious poverty.
Juvenal

At thirty, a man suspects himself a fool; Knows it
at forty, and reforms his plan; At fifty chides his
infamous delay,
Pushes his prudent purpose to resolve; In all the
magnanimity of thought Resolves, and re-
resolves; then dies the same.
Edward Young

The vitality of thought is an adventure. Ideas
won't keep. Something must be done about
them. When the idea is new, its custodians have
fervor, live for it, and, if need be, die for it.
Alfred North Whitehead

Beware of all enterprises that require new
clothes.
Henry David Thoreau

Ideas don't make you rich. The correct execution
of ideas does.
Felix Dennis

We are the music-makers,
And we are the dreamers of dreams,
Wandering by lone sea breakers,
And sitting by desolate streams;
World-losers, and world-forsakers,
On whom the pale moon gleams;
Yet we are the movers and shakers
Of the World forever, it seems.
Arthur O'Shaughnessy

Nothing is more dangerous than an idea, when
it's the only one we have.
Emile Auguste Chartier

It is better to be making the news than taking it;
to be an actor rather than a critic.
Sir Winston Churchill

He that will not apply new remedies must expect
new evils; for time is the greatest innovator.
Francis Bacon

One of the greatest pains to human nature is the
pain of a new idea.
Walter Bagehot

I seen my opportunities and I took 'em.
George Washington Plunkitt

No bird soars too high, if he soars with his wings.
Wlliam Blake

Many times we will get more ideas and better
ideas in two hours of creative loafing than in
eight hours at a desk.
Wilfred Peterson

The rewards in business go to the man who does
something with an idea.
William Benton

When you are going through Hell, keep going.
Sir Winston Churchill

You are the one who must choose his place.
James Lane Allen

Life shrinks or expands in proportion to one's
courage.
Anaïs Nin

After all, tomorrow is another day.
Margaret Mitchell
We are continually faced by great opportunities
brilliantly disguised as insoluble problems.
Lee Iacocca

The secret of getting ahead is getting started. The secret of getting started is breaking your complex overwhelming tasks into small manageable tasks, and then starting on the first one.
Mark Twain

I owe my success to having listened respectfully to the very best advice, and then going away and doing the exact opposite.
G K Chesterton

Don't think of it as failure, think of it as time-released success.
Robert Orben

One machine can do the work of fifty ordinary men. No machine can do the work of one extraordinary man.
Elbert Hubbard

Most people can do extraordinary things if they have the confidence or take risks. Yet most people don't. They sit in front of the TV and treat life as if it goes on forever.
Philip Adams

No matter how big or soft or warm your bed is,
you still have to get out of it.
Grace Slick

Writers are really people who write books not
because they are poor, but because they are
dissatisfied with the books which they could buy
but do not like.
Walter Benjamin

You should hammer your iron while it is hot.
Publius Syrus

And the trouble is, if you don't risk anything, you
risk even more.
Erica Jong

To be successful, the first thing you do is fall in
love with your work.
Mary Lauretta

Business is like sex. When it's good, it's very,
very good; when it's not so good, it's still good.
George Katona

People have a way of becoming what you encourage them to be – not what you nag them to be.
S. N Parker

If you can meet with Triumph and Disaster
And treat those two imposters the same…
If you can talk with crowds and keep your virtue,
Or walk with Kings – nor lose the common touch…
Yours is the Earth and everything that's in it,
And –which is more – you'll be a man, my son!
Rudyard Kipling

But I would not give in. And that was the secret ingredient. I would not be a wage slave. I would not take "no' for an answer. I would not give in. I was going to be rich. Somehow. Some way. Someday soon. And I would not retreat to the safety of a decent job until I was starved out of house and home. I would not give in.
Felix Dennis

A hero is a man who does what he can.
Romain Rolland

To fight a bull when you are not scared is
nothing. And to *not* fight a bull when you are
scared is nothing. But to fight a bull when you
are scared is something.
Anon.

To establish oneself in the world, one has to do
all one can to appear established.
Francois de la Rochefoucault

There are risks and costs to a program of action.
But they are far less than the long-range risks
and costs of comfortable inaction.
John F Kennedy

When I talked, no one listened to me. But as
soon as I acted I became persuasive, and I no
longer find anyone incredulous.
Giosue Borsi

The only things you regret are the things you
didn't do.
Michael Curtiz

Conditions are never just right. People who delay
action until all factors are favorable do nothing.
William Feather

Having a dream isn't stupid. It's not having a dream that's stupid.
Anon.

Unless you enter the tiger's lair, you cannot take the cubs.
Japanese Proverb

Success is that old ABC – Ability, Breaks and Courage.
Charles Luckman

I've been polite and I've always shown up. Somebody asked me if I had any advice for young people entering the business. I said "Yeah, show up."
Tom T Hall

Great Books
to Read

"The Entrepreneurial Spirit", A. David Silver.

"Zen and the Art of Making a Living : A Practical Guide to Creative Career Design", Laurence G. Boldt

"Begin it now", Susan Hayward.

"The Artist's Way: A Spiritual Path to Higher Creativity", Julia Cameron.

"From Zero to Hero," Charles Banfe

"The Naked Entrepreneur", David Robinson

"The Leader: A New Face for American Management," Michael Maccoby

"The Charismatic Leader : Behind the Mystique of Exceptional Leadership",Jay Alden Conger.

"Living Juicy : Daily Morsels for Your Creative Soul", Sark.

"Feel the Fear and Do It Anyway", Susan Jeffers

"The Psychology of Winning," Denis Waitley

"Seeds of Greatness," Denis Waitley

"On Becoming a Leader," Warren Bennis

"Creativity in Business," Michael Ray & Rochelle Myers.

"Think and Grow Rich," Napoleon Hill.

"New Venture Strategies," Karl Vesper.

"Corporate Darwinism," Warren Avis et al.

"The Art of the Start: The Time-Tested, Battle-Hardened Guide for Anyone Starting Anything", Guy Kawasaki.

"Success Through A Positive Mental Attitude," Napoleon Hill and W Clement Stone.

Other Quotations websites:
http://www.minterest.com/99-inspirational-motivational-quotes-on-entrepreneurship/

http://work-at-home-based-business.com/2010/01/04/50-success-quotes-for-entrepreneurs/

http://businessnoob.com/26-inspirational-quotes-for-the-aspiring-entrepreneur/

(Jack Burkhart is a pseudonym.)